God Talk

13 Things Everybody Needs to Know About God

by Lee Hotchkiss

Edited by Chuck Peters
Book Design by Chris Gates

www.leehotchkiss.com

Table of Contents

Section V – The Church and Strategic Equipping

God Talk
13 Things Everybody Needs to Know About God

Introduction

Meaningful talk about God is the most important communication that we can have. Why is God talk important? It is important because it honors God. He is the most important and glorious being in the universe and we are commissioned to teach and make disciples that know, love and follow him.[1] Meaningful God talk must be biblically accurate, clear, and appropriate for the situation. It's also important because it deals with the eternal destiny of souls. The Lord's commission to go everywhere and make disciples continues today and is binding upon every believer. It is not optional. We are commanded to bear witness of him and his message of redemption. We are called to speak about this most glorious subject that has eternal significance.

Clear God talk is important because we are called to honor him though obedient witness about him as he draws people to himself. We must be diligent to speak words that make this news understandable. Our words do not cause a person to believe the message that Jesus Christ came into the world to reveal God, to die on a cross to take away sin, and to provide the way for people to know him. God himself communicates the message to the sinner's heart as the Holy Spirit reveals truth to the mind and draws a

---

1   Matthew 28:18-20

person to the Savior.[2] But God has chosen to use imperfect humans. We are called to faithfully share the good news and he does what we cannot do. It is not the cleverness of our words that causes a person to believe the message, but God's mysterious work of the Holy Spirit in bringing about the new birth.[3] Our job is simply to share the message in an honest, straightforward and accurate way and then pray that God will bring a spiritual harvest.

Often overlooked is the fact that the redemptive work of Christ is anchored in the very nature of God. At its very core the gospel is about the person and work of Jesus Christ - two subjects that belong together.[4] A common trend in witnessing, however, is to focus mostly on the work of Christ and to say little about the person of Christ and the nature of God. Many today hesitate to communicate a full-bodied message about who God is. I believe that is a mistake. It is the aim of this book to assist and better equip ordinary people to speak more clearly, more confidently and more robustly about God.

Peter said that we should be prepared to give an answer whenever people ask about our hope.[5] We must be ready to speak truth clearly with gentleness and respect. People are looking for something to fill their spiritual vacuums, yet many have grown leery of the traditional church. A recent article in USA Weekend magazine entitled "How Americans Imagine God"[6] illustrates the general shallowness of public thought about God. It demonstrates that many prefer to

2   2 Corinthians 3:16 and John 6:37-40, 44
3   John 3:3-8
4   1 Corinthians 2:2
5   1 Peter 3:15
6   Cathy Lynn Grossman, USA Weekend (McLean, VA: A Gannett publication, December 17-19, 2010), p.6.

pick and choose ideas from various sources. This approach is appealing because it puts them in control. It allows them to be creative as they indulge in speculative thinking about spiritual matters. When they design their own god, they can choose from a mixture of features taken from eastern religions, sentimental family traditions, classical Greek or Roman mythology, comic book superheroes or favorite movie theme. This eclectic approach to thinking about God may be hopelessly naïve, but it is attractive to many within our consumer culture. It is rich in fantasy, but short on reality. Reading the hundreds of responses to the USA Weekend article online was fascinating. Many people are quick to spout-off about their views. Opportunities for engaging in significant God talk abound. This is especially true, as the article stated, during "spiritual seasons" of the year. Heightened interest in the spiritual also happens when a person's worldview is being tested by personal experiences of distress.

It is into this dynamic, and increasingly post-Christian, arena of confusion that we must speak. No wonder so many followers of Jesus Christ are uncertain about how to communicate their beliefs. I believe the solution begins by learning to sharpen our thinking about God so we can speak more clearly and accurately about him. We need to organize and summarize our thoughts in a way that is memorable so that we can speak with confidence when we have opportunity to talk about God with real people in real life situations.

God Talk outlines thirteen things that everyone needs to know about God, organized using simple memory hooks to help you recall them when you are asked to give a reason for your faith so you can answer without groping for words. The outline is simple and the content is biblical. Each point is anchored in Scripture. Each point is scalable and flexible, to prepare you to give a brief overview in a few seconds or to expand a point in greater detail.

This book does not attempt to be all-inclusive or a comprehensive theology or apologetic that answers every question. It is deliberately brief. *God Talk* is designed to be a tool for use by busy people who desire to have significant conversations about God while doing life on the run. It is, rather, a practical summary that attempts to provide a simple outline to aid your memory by linking key thoughts together into a logical overview.

It also helps with the problem of balance. Hobbyhorse theology tends to be lopsided because it focuses on favorite topics about God but excludes other essential information. We are left with descriptions of God that feel like an out-of-round tire on the freeway, distracting and uncomfortable to the listener, but also dangerous. They dishonor God because they present a caricature or an inadequate view of who he is. Our desire should be to stay balanced in our God talk. Remember imbalance often leads to heresy. A. W. Tozer writing fifty years ago in his classic book The Knowledge of the Holy said, "The low view of God entertained almost universally among Christians is the cause of a hundred lesser evils everywhere among us."[7]

The memory hooks will ease your fear of getting lost in the many details of this enormous subject. They provide you with points of reference to which you can return when your conversation gets sidetracked, so you can remember where you are in a logical presentation about who God is. I am not suggesting that you draw attention to the memory

---

7   A. W. Tozer, *The Knowledge of the Holy*
(New York: Harper & Row, 1961), p.5.

aids but rather use them discretely to help you in your own thought process. Your communication should be about God not the memory hooks. If you do show them to the person you are speaking with, simply explain that they help you remember important truths about God. Sharing them in a family setting can be helpful to teach children important truth. People of all ages can enjoy learning along with you as you practice and increase your skill at God talk.

Section I
Big Ideas About God

1
God is Above and Beyond Creation

Memory Hook - Move your hand out, up and away.

Does God live in a building or temple? Must we make a pilgrimage to encounter him? Where is he? What is he like? These are common questions that are raised when the subject of God comes up and it is a good place to begin.

God is spirit and exists everywhere.[8] But he is not part of the universe. He is infinite and limitless. The word transcendence is used to explain that he exists above and beyond the creation. The Bible speaks about a place where God dwells and calls it heaven. It is a holy place, the location of his temple and the throne from which he rules.[9] The apostle John described a vision of heaven in the book of Revelation where God was seated on his throne in heaven as a place of awesome beauty, flashing lightning, peals of thunder, brilliant colors and myriads of adoring spiritual beings singing praises.[10] This is a real place from where his authority and glory radiate (even though some

---

8   John 4:24

9   Psalm 2:4 "The One enthroned in heaven laughs;" 11:4 "The Lord is in his holy temple; the Lord is on his heavenly throne." and 103:19 "The Lord has established his throne in heaven and his kingdom rules over all."

10   Revelation 4:2-6

of the description may be symbolic) - a place of which our deepest and grandest thoughts cannot adequately conceive. Language fails to describe the abode of the awesome living God of the Bible.

A common response when men encountered God in the Bible was to fall to the ground in fear and awe. Moses was cautioned to remove his sandals and keep his distance.[11] When Moses met with God on Mount Sinai the people were warned to stay back or face death.[12] Ezekiel fell facedown in response to seeing a vision of God that left him reeling.[13] Isaiah cried out "Woe to me!" after seeing the Lord seated on a throne high and exalted. He gained a new awareness of his sinful condition in comparison to the holiness of God that caused him to say, "I am ruined!"[14] The writer of the book of Hebrews warns worshipers to approach God with reverence and awe because, he says, "God is a consuming fire."[15] God is truly awesome.

King David had planned to build a house for God. At the dedication of the temple in Jerusalem, Solomon said, "But will God really dwell on earth? The heavens, even the highest heaven, cannot contain you. How much less this temple I have built!"[16] Solomon understood that God is not limited to a specific location or any sacred building. God is spirit and transcendent.

Jesus spoke comfort to the disciples about his Father's house having many rooms and that he was going to prepare

---

11   Exodus 3:5
12   Exodus 19:12-13
13   Ezekiel 1:1-28
14   Isaiah 6:1-5
15   Hebrews 12:28-29
16   1 Kings 8:27

a place for them.[17] We long to be with him enjoying that special place that he has prepared for us in God's presence. Like the heroes of faith listed in Hebrews chapter eleven, we anticipate a heavenly city, a place prepared and made ready to enjoy sweet fellowship with God in his heavenly home. But God also says that he dwells with us now! We will explore this truth in chapter two.

The simple memory hook, (a wave of the hand out, up and away) helps us remember this first fundamental and profound truth about God. It reminds us that God is above and beyond all creation.

God exists outside of creation, but he exists. God is and is self-existent. God is, and he is transcendent. He is above and beyond the creation. He is separate from the universe and not limited to it or dependent upon it. He is the God who exists outside of time. God is spirit, eternal and changeless.[18]

He disclosed himself to Moses with these words, "I AM WHO I AM."[19] The name Yahweh or Jehovah is found approximately 5,321 times in the Old Testament.[20] J. I. Packer says, "This 'name' is not a description of God, but simply a declaration of His self-existence, and His eternal changelessness; a reminder to mankind that He has life in Himself, and that what He is now, He is eternally."[21]

---

17   John 14:2-3
18   Deuteronomy 33:27; Psalm 90:2; Romans 16:26
19   Exodus 3:14
20   Charles C. Ryrie, *Basic Theology*
      (Wheaton: Victor Books, 1987), p. 47.
21   J. I. Packer, *Knowing God*
      (Downers Grove, IL: InterVarsity Press, 1973), p. 69.

Man was created in God's image. While we share something of his likeness, we do not share his transcendence. God is distinct and separate from anything in the created order (including angels). The purpose of the first three of the Ten Commandments protects God's holy separateness. There were to be no other gods, no idols of created things and no misuse of his sacred name.[22] God is solely worthy of man's worship as stated in the greatest commandment, to love the Lord God with our whole being.[23] Twice in the book of Revelation the Apostle John had to be reminded not to worship an angel.[24]

We should stop at this point and think about how large segments of the world's population worship various aspects of creation. There are many ancient traditions of people worshiping the sun, moon and stars. Today there are many who speak of the universe as having intelligence and god-like characteristics while denying the God of creation. Ecological concern (in some quarters) even reaches to the level of earth-worship. There is a growing tendency to equate the universe with god, not unlike the older pantheism that saw god in all material things. In animistic societies evil spirits are worshipped, feared and appeased. These spirits are thought to inhabit rocks, trees and other objects of creation. All this underscores the importance of beginning our God talk with the truth that God is, is spirit and is transcendent. He is above and beyond creation, not part of it or dependent upon it in any way.

---

22   Exodus 20:3-7
23   Matthew 22:36-38
24   Revelation 19:10; 22:8-9

2
God is Personal

> *Memory Hook - Point your index finger back toward your heart.*

God is transcendent but he is also personal.[25] He desires to relate to you and me personally. It is amazing but true. The infinite God wants to have an intimate relationship with you, a finite individual person.

"For this is what the high and lofty One says – he who lives forever, whose name is holy: 'I live in a high and holy place, but also with him who is contrite and lowly in spirit.'"[26] In the New Testament Jesus said these astounding words. "If anyone loves me, he will obey my teaching. My Father will love him, and we will come to him and make our home with him."[27] What awesome statements. God, the most holy and exalted One is willing to dwell with the contrite and lowly in spirit, with those who love and obey him.

God is a person who thinks, feels and acts. The three persons of the Godhead; the Father, the Son and the Holy Spirit are one, but exist in three persons. The members of the Trinity relate in perfect harmonious and intimate

25   D. A. Carson,
The Gagging of God: Christianity Confronts Pluralism
(Grand Rapid, Zondervan Publishing, 1996), p. 223.
26   Isaiah 57:15
27   John 14:23

communication.[28] Man was created in the image and
likeness of God.[29] We are moral beings with a capacity
to think, feel and act. These capacities were damaged
in the fall. This continues to affect how we relate in our
personal relationships. The degree and extent to which
these capacities were damaged continues to be a significant
discussion among theologians. It also explains why we have
such difficulty in human relationships.

The Bible is filled with examples of God revealing himself
to man for the purpose of relationship, and sometimes
speaks of people "walking" together with God or being in
the presence of God. It says of Enoch that he walked with
God.[30] And when Abraham was ninety-nine years old, "the
Lord appeared to him and said, 'I am God Almighty; walk
before me and be blameless.'"[31] In the New Testament Jesus
spoke an invitation through John to the church at Laodicea.
"Here I am! I stand at the door and knock. If anyone hears
my voice and opens the door, I will come in and eat with
him, and he with me."[32] The picture of eating is an ancient
way of describing intimate fellowship and close personal
relationship.

Jesus said, "I am the good shepherd; I know my sheep
and my sheep know me."[33] He also spoke to the disciples
about the Holy Spirit in relational terms, "But you know
him, for he lives with you and will be in you"[34] and praying
to the Father said, "I want those you have given me to be

28	John 10:30; 12:49-50
29	Genesis 1:26-27; 2:7
30	Genesis 5:24
31	Genesis 17:1
32	Revelation 3:20
33	John 10:14
34	John 14:17

with me where I am …I have made you known to them, and will continue to make you known in order that the love you have for me may be in them and that I myself may be in them."[35] The Apostle Paul wrote that his great passion was to know Christ.[36] The reader can sense that he was not speaking about some dry, dusty, theoretical concept but about an intimate, vibrant, personal relationship with the living God. God is personal, and he desires to relate to you and me personally.

---

35   John 17:24-26
36   Philippians 3:8, 10

3
God Speaks

Memory Hook – Move your hand up to your lips.

God has spoken in the past and he continues to speak in many ways. "In the past God spoke to our forefathers through the prophets at many times and in various ways, but in these last days he has spoken to us by his Son."[37] The ultimate revelation of God is found in the incarnation of his Son, the Lord Jesus Christ. Paul said that, "He is the image of the invisible God"[38] and that "God was pleased to have all his fullness dwell in him."[39] The writer of the book of Hebrews adds, "The Son is the radiance of God's glory and the exact representation of his being."[40]

Psalm 19 is eloquent about how the creation clearly proclaims the glory of God and how the written Law is effective in communicating God's divine truth. God's written word is very special communication. It is "inspired," or God-breathed.[41] Speaking through Isaiah, God said that his word will accomplish its purpose.[42] Jesus adds, "I tell you the truth, until heaven and earth disappear, not the smallest letter, not

---

37 Hebrews 1:1-2
38 Colossians 1:15
39 Colossians 1:19
40 Hebrews 1:3
41 2 Timothy 3:16
42 Isaiah 55:11

the least stroke of a pen, will by any means disappear from the Law until everything is accomplished."[43]

Jesus said that his sheep listen to his voice.[44] God is an effective communicator. He can use other means of communication such as dreams (common in the Old Testament and also a frequent testimony today among believers coming to faith in Christ from an Islamic background) and through other special circumstances, but Scripture (the Bible) is his primary method by which he speaks today.[45]

J. I. Packer states, "Not only is Scripture the fountainhead for knowledge of God, Christ and salvation, but it presents this knowledge in an incomparably vivid, powerful and evocative way. The canonical Scriptures are a veritable book of life ... Still, through the records of His earthly ministry, the quickening voice of Christ Himself is heard. Still, through the written word, He speaks..."[46]

God speaks. And what he speaks is true and trustworthy. When God speaks, we should pay attention.

---

43   Matthew 5:18

44   John 10:27

45   Acts 9:3-6; Hebrews 4:12; Romans 10:17

46   J. I. Packer, *God Has Spoken*
(Downers Grove, IL: IV Press, 1979), pp. 13-14.

From Presuppositions to Attributes

We will pick up the concept of God being trustworthy in the next chapter, but first let me share some thoughts in transition to Section Two, which deals with the attributes of God. Section One lays a foundation of big ideas that serve as a starting point in God talk. These presuppositions, or foundational assumptions, include the belief that God exists, is transcendent yet personal and has spoken. The atheist begins with the presupposition that God does not exist. If a person wants to argue the existence of God, we quickly move from the arena of basic witness to apologetics, which is beyond the purpose of this book. It is good, however, to have a logical answer for the person who asks why you believe these things.

You must resist the fear that comes from believing that you must prove that God exists. This can paralyze you and prevent you from speaking a witness of what you believe. It is important to remember that it is God's design to require faith when it comes to approaching God. "And without faith it is impossible to please God, because anyone who comes to him must believe that he exists and that he rewards those who earnestly seek him."[47]

Wise theology begins with the uncomfortable truth that man is limited in his knowledge. It is not possible for us to adequately define, describe or defend God, as he is transcendent and beyond our finite grasp. He is unknowable, apart from his gracious willingness to disclose himself. Tozer's chapter titled, "God Incomprehensible" is a good discussion on this subject.[48]

---

47   Hebrews 11:6
48   Tozer, p. 12.

Biblical Christianity is not a blind leap of faith but a belief that what God has revealed is true. We can know truth about God through the Bible (God's special revelation), the creation (natural revelation), and the incarnation of Jesus Christ. Humility and faith must permeate our God talk. Humility because we don't have all the answers and faith because we remember that Jesus said, "No one knows the Son except the Father, and no one knows the Father except the Son and those to whom the Son chooses to reveal him."[49] Our God talk must be bathed in prayer that God will do a supernatural work through our simple words of witness.

In Section Two we turn to the subject of the attributes, or perfections, of God.[50] Charles C. Ryrie in his Basic Theology, devotes chapter six to the "The Perfections of God." He discusses how the attributes of God are generally classified into categories such as natural and moral, absolute and relative, and incommunicable and communicable.[51] He then proceeds to assemble a catalog of fourteen perfections of God. His list includes: eternity, freedom, immutability, infinity, holiness, love, omnipotence, omnipresence,

---

49   Matthew 11:27

50   J. I. Packer, *Knowing God* (Downers Grove, IL: IV Press, 1973), p. 16.

51   According to Ryrie, God's non-moral or natural attributes "like his self-existence and infinity, belong to the constitution of God" and the moral attributes are qualities "like justice and holiness." "Absolute attributes include those which belong to the essence of God as considered in itself (eternity, infinity), and relative attributes belong to the essence of God as considered in relation to His creation (like omniscience)." Incommunicable attributes "are those which belong only to God (eternity, infinity), while [communicable] are those which are found in a relative or limited degree in people (wisdom, justice)." Charles C. Ryrie, *Basic Theology* (Wheaton: Victor Books, 1987), p. 36.

omniscience, righteousness, simplicity, sovereignty, truth and unity.[52]

I have found it helpful to compile a shorter list from these and other long lists of attributes.[53] By summarizing them into similar themes, five logical groups or clusters emerge. These five groups of perfections will form the outline of Section II of this book.

God is perfect. In the Sermon on the Mount Jesus said that God is perfect.[54] This is true in regard to anything that we say about God. When the Bible reveals that God is righteous, we must realize that he is perfectly righteous. This is why I prefer the term perfections (plural) to describe God. It reminds me that he is perfect in all aspects of his nature, attributes and character. We should also note that all of the attributes of God apply equally and perfectly to each of the three persons of the Trinity.

---

52   Ibid., pp. 36-44.

53   Many attempts have been made to put together lists of the most salient characteristics of God's nature and attributes. The Westminster Shorter Catechism, question four asks; "What is God? Answer: God is a Spirit, infinite, eternal and unchangeable, in his being, wisdom, power, holiness, justice, goodness, and truth." The Westminster Larger Catechism expands that list in question seven answering: "God is a Spirit, in and of Himself infinite in being, glory, blessedness, and perfection; all-sufficient, eternal, unchangeable, incomprehensible, everywhere present, almighty; knowing all things, most wise, most holy, most just, most merciful and gracious, long-suffering, and abundant in goodness and truth." Brian W. Kinny, ed., *The Confessions of Our Faith* (Fortress Book Service and Publishers, 2007), p. 59 and 124.

54   Matthew 5:48

Section II
The Attributes of God

4
God is Truth

> *Memory Hook - The ring finger reminds us of keeping promises. Move your right hand to touch the finger where a wedding band is placed. God is a covenant keeping God who is trustworthy and faithfully keeps his promises.*

What is God like as a person? He is trustworthy. He keeps his word, his covenants and promises. The first group of the perfections of God is therefore the truth cluster. It includes the fact that God is true, speaks truth, and is trustworthy and faithful. He can be trusted.

Jesus embodied truth. Jesus said, "I am the truth."[55] John said of Jesus, "The Word became flesh and made his dwelling among us. We have seen his glory, the glory of the One and Only, who came from the Father, full of grace and truth" and "grace and truth came through Jesus Christ"[56]

When God disclosed himself to Moses at Mt. Sinai we are told that he is "abounding in love and faithfulness."[57] David spoke of the trustworthy nature of God's word when he said, "The judgments of the Lord are true; they

---

55   John 14:6

56   John 1:14; 17

57   Exodus 34:5-6 NASB reads "lovingkindness and truth"

are righteous altogether."[58] These examples illustrate how the Hebrew word "true" often carries the idea of faithful, trustworthy and sure. Also, "the faithfulness of the Lord endures forever"[59] and "the word of the Lord is right and true; he is faithful in all he does."[60]

The concept of God making promises and being faithful to his word is an important part of this cluster. "God, who does not lie, promised before the beginning of time"[61] and "When God made his promise to Abraham, since there was no one greater for him to swear by, he swore by himself" and "Because God wanted to make the unchanging nature of his purpose very clear... he confirmed it with an oath... it is impossible for God to lie."[62] These statements echo the statement in the Psalms that "all your words are true"[63] and Jesus declaration that "heaven and earth will pass away, but my words will never pass away,"[64] and his statement while praying to the Father, "Sanctify them by the truth; your word is truth."[65]

I have quoted a number of verses here to show how important this concept is in the Bible. The trustworthiness of what God has spoken is an essential part in a person's coming to faith in Christ. From the human point of view a person must believe that God is truthful and trustworthy. The Bible testifies that he is. We can add our witness to how God has been faithful to us in our life experience.

---

58   Psalm 19:9 NASB, NIV reads "sure"
59   Psalm 117:2 NASB reads "the truth of the Lord is everlasting"
60   Psalm 33:4
61   Titus 1:2
62   Hebrews 6:13; 17-18
63   Psalm 119:160
64   Luke 21:33
65   John 17:17

5
God is Sovereign

Memory Hook - Grasp your thumb. As the strongest of the digits, the thumb reminds me of God's sovereignty.

I call the second group of perfections the sovereignty cluster. This group includes the truth that God is all-knowing (omniscience), all-powerful (omnipotence), and is the Almighty, the sovereign ruler of heaven and earth. The Bible speaks of this cluster of attributes of God from beginning to end and it is a major theme of the Bible. Tozer wrote, "God's sovereignty is the attribute by which He rules His entire creation, and to be sovereign God must be all-knowing, all-powerful, and absolutely free."[66]

Another term that has been used to describe this cluster is the word providence. The Heidelberg Catechism, question twenty seven asked: "What dost thou mean by the providence of God? Answer: The almighty and everywhere present power of God; whereby, as it were by his hand, he upholds and governs heaven, earth, and all creatures; so that herbs and grass, rain and drought, fruitful and barren years, meat and drink, health and sickness, riches and poverty, yea, and all things come, not by chance, but by his fatherly

---

66   A. W. Tozer, *The Knowledge of the Holy*
(New York: Harper and Row, Publishers, 1961), p. 115.

hand."[67] The language may seem a little stiff for our day, but the message is clear - God is sovereign and in control.

One biblical passage that speaks plainly regarding this is the book of Daniel. In chapter two Nebuchadnezzar, the king of Babylon, was told through a dream that he stood at the head of a short list of kings who would rule the whole known world. In the dream he saw a statue that represented four world empires. His kingdom was the dazzling statue's head of gold. God disclosed that Nebuchadnezzar was to have the most glorious and powerful empire of the four. In chapter four we hear Nebuchadnezzar's testimony, a confession of how he became filled with pride and how the Most High God, the sovereign ruler and Lord of heaven took away Nebuchadnezzar's sanity and his kingdom for seven years until he acknowledged "that the Most High is sovereign over the kingdoms of men and gives them to anyone he wishes."[68]

God provides two things in this passage; an overview of world political history, and a strong statement of his sovereignty over the political empires of man and those who rule them. It is a shame that many people only remember the story of chapter three about Shadrach, Meshach and Abednego and the blazing furnace but miss the major truth that God is sovereign over all things.

The theme of God's sovereign rule is often repeated in Scripture. Here is a sample from the Psalms. "He rules forever by his power. For the Lord is a great God, the great King above all the earth. The Lord is exalted over all the nations, his glory above the heavens. Who is like the Lord

---

67   The Christian Classics Ethereal Library (CCEL).
http://www.ccel.org/creeds/heidelberg-cat-ext.txt
68   Daniel 4:25

our God, the One who sits enthroned on high…? Our God is in heaven; he does whatever pleases him. The earth is the Lord's and everything in it, the world, and all who live in it; Who is he, this King of glory? The Lord Almighty – he is the King of glory."[69]

These statements and many others speak of God's sovereign rule. Note how these are found in a context of praise or celebration of God. Praise and worship most often occur when God's people begin to understand and reflect upon some attribute of God. James Montgomery Boice put it this way. "God's glory consists of his intrinsic worth embodied in his character, and that the acknowledgment of this worth by those who are his people is worship."[70]

When we catch a glimpse of God's sovereignty, we are catching a glimpse of God's glory. Worship is acknowledging his sovereignty (his right to rule), bowing to it, and praising him for who he is, what he has done, what he is doing in the present and what he has promised to do in the future.

We are called to bear witness to God's sovereign rule as it is part of the gospel. In the New Testament this is often expressed as preaching the gospel of the kingdom of God where Christ rules in all things. Christian worship begins to come alive and make sense when this truth is understood. Note the beautiful words of worship found in Psalm 147 that speak of God's power and care for the humbled and broken. "Praise the Lord. How good it is to sing praises to our God, how pleasant and fitting to praise him! He heals the brokenhearted and binds up their wounds. He determines the number of the stars and calls them each by name. Great

---

69   Psalm 66:7; 95:3, 113:4-5; 115:3; 24:1 and 10
70   James Montgomery Boice, *The Gospel of John*, Vol. 4, (Grand Rapids: Baker Books, 1985), p. 1032.

is our Lord and mighty in power; his understanding has no limit. The Lord sustains the humble."[71]

It is often when we are the most challenged and crushed by circumstances in life that the truth of God's sovereign control and care become most precious to us. It is in this arena where faith and prayer are exercised and grow vibrant. As we bear witness to God's sovereignty we ultimately are inviting people to cry out to God for his mercy and grace. We may be speaking to a person that God, in his sovereignty, has been bringing to a point of brokenness and despair through some set of circumstances that we know nothing about. It is here, in real life events, that we often begin to learn about the sovereignty cluster. An important part of trusting God is learning to pray, asking for God's intervention and trusting his will to be done. It is important (and humbling) to remember that God's sovereign will is unknowable until it happens or until he discloses it. God is truly sovereign.

---

71   Psalm 147:1, 3-6

6
God is Righteous

> *Memory Hook - The memory hook for this cluster is the index finger. In many parts to the world pointing with this finger is accusatory. It reminds me that God is holy, righteous and just, but I am not.*

The third group of the perfections of God is the righteousness cluster. This group includes the truth that God is holy, pure, righteous and just. The sheer volume of usage of these words in the Bible is vast. Their combined occurrence numbers well over one thousand.

In speaking with Moses, God attributed holiness to himself when he said, "I am holy."[72] In Isaiah's vision of God the heavenly beings called out, "Holy, holy, holy is the Lord Almighty."[73] And in John's vision of heaven he writes that the living creatures, never stop in their adoration of God, saying, "Holy, holy, holy is the Lord God Almighty."[74] Psalm ninety nine asserts God's holiness three times and plainly states that "God is holy."[75]

The word holy carries the idea of moral purity, being undefiled, set apart and sacred. Holiness is often closely

---

72   Leviticus 11:44
73   Isaiah 6:3
74   Revelation 4:8
75   Psalm 99:3, 5 and 9

related to God's glory and represented as brilliant light. The word righteousness is used frequently in the context of God dealing with man. "He will judge the world in righteousness and the peoples with equity."[76] The gospel is also framed in terms of God's righteousness being revealed and provided to the believer.[77] This is foundational to a biblical understanding of the gospel. The Holy Spirit many times begins to convict a person of their need of the gospel when we faithfully share who God is in this righteousness cluster.[78]

The Bible says that "righteousness and justice are the foundation" of God's throne and that he "loves righteousness and justice."[79] The Bible is clear that God's rule of the earth is from his throne in heaven and that all he does is righteous, holy and just.[80] Satan commonly sows seeds of mistrust trying to undermine people's perception of God's character. God is perfectly righteous, holy and just, and we are to bear witness of this important truth about him.

---

76   Psalm 98:9
77   Romans 1:17; 3:21-22
78   John 16:8-11
79   Psalm 89:14; Psalm 33:5
80   Psalm 9:7-8

7
God is Love

Memory Hook - The memory hook for God's love is the large middle finger. It reminds me of God's great love that shows in his kindness and compassion. Yes, we live in a fallen world that has turned the raised middle finger into a symbol of hate and vulgarity, but I am reminded of how opposite and pure God's love is compared to the twisted vile abuse and corruption man displays without God.

The fourth cluster of perfections includes the truth that God is loving, kind, gentle and compassionate. The Apostle John seemed to have special insight into this attribute. He described himself as "the disciple whom Jesus loved."[81] John wrote about this profound truth of God's love in the simplest way by stating, "God is love"[82] He continued on to explain how God showed his love to us by sending his Son into the world to provide salvation.[83]

Much has been said about the sacrificial aspect of agape love, which seeks what is best for the one loved. How it desires to provide benefit for the other by taking action

---

81   John 13:23
82   1 John 4:8, 16
83   1 John 4:9; John 3:16

at personal expense. As important as this concept is for understanding love, the subject is wider and includes honor, respect and cherishing the other. It is a warm relational term that includes expression, communication, and fellowship. Perfect love and communication takes place within the Trinity.[84] The Bible speaks extensively about love between God and his people[85] and of how love is to be the identifying mark among God's people.[86]

Other words that belong in this cluster include kindness, goodness and mercy. The kindness of God in Scripture is often linked with salvation, and points to God's love in action toward those in need.[87]

The gentleness or meekness of God is closely associated with his kindness. David speaks of it as how God dealt with him, "Thy gentleness makes me great."[88] Jesus described himself as being "gentle and humble in heart."[89] Paul also referred to the "meekness and gentleness of Christ" in how he appealed to the church in Corinth.[90]

The compassion of God is closely associated with his love and mercy. The Hebrew word *racham* is translated as both mercy and compassion.[91] These concepts clearly overlap and it may be somewhat arbitrary to draw a line between them, but for the sake of this outline we will develop mercy and grace in the next cluster. Matthew comments on Jesus

---

84   John 17:23-26
85   Ephesians 3:18-19; 2 Thessalonians 2:16; 2 Corinthians 13:14
86   1 John 4:20-21; John 13:34; 1 Corinthians 13
87   Ephesians 2:7; Titus 3:4; 1 Peter 2:3
88   Psalm 18:35(NASB)
89   Matthew 11:29
90   2 Corinthians 10:1
91   Psalm 25:6 (NIV "mercy" and NASB "compassion")

being moved with compassion four times.[92] In each case he sees people in need, feels pity for them and takes action to help them. God is truly love, and he is full of compassion, kindness and gentleness.

---

92   Matthew 9:36; 14:14; 15:32; 20:34

8
God is Gracious

Memory Hook - The memory hook for this cluster is the little finger, which reminds me of my weakness, and need of God's mercy and grace.

Last in the five clusters of the perfections of God is grace. This group includes the truth that God is gracious, full of mercy and lovingkindness. One of the most important words of the Old Testament is the Hebrew word *chesed*. It is found 249 times and means goodness, kindness and faithfulness. It is often translated mercy, kindness, love and lovingkindness. Theologians speak of this word expressing God's covenant love.

The Psalms reverberate with prayers pleading for God's mercy and praise from those who received it.[93] It is one of the richest themes in Scripture. God is good to rescue those who cry out to him for mercy when they are in trouble and distress.

The New Testament favors the word grace and refers to God's unmerited favor spoken of as a gift. The word grace is found 114 times. It is used most extensively by Paul as he develops the doctrine of the grace of God in salvation through Jesus Christ. Anchored in and motivated by God's

93   Psalm 13:5; 25:6-7; 51:1

love, his grace is rich in mercy, providing salvation by faith.[94] Paul's emphasis on salvation by grace through faith is clearly contrasted with religious systems that teach the futile attempt to gain righteousness through good works and self-effort.[95] God is merciful and gracious.

94   Ephesians 2:4-9
95   Titus 3:5-7; Romans 5:1-2

Celebrating the Perfections of God in Private Worship

Before moving on to Section Three to explore the actions of God for the purpose of witness, let me pause for a moment to suggest another application of this section. I have personally experienced a growing desire to explore the nature and character of God both in my study and devotional life. The more I study the perfections of God the more I find myself drawn to celebrate them, and delight in him, in my private worship. This has helped me become more God-centered in my personal time of worship.

I encourage you to use the five-cluster approach in your time alone with God. As you use it in private worship you will find that your confidence will grow in speaking with others. It will become more natural to think and speak about the perfections of God. This simple five-point structure will provide a foundation for launching out in greater detail and more expansive breadth as you add more Scriptural content on the subject of each cluster. You will also begin to experience a new freedom to meditate and praise while driving, walking, sitting or kneeling with your eyes open or closed. I encourage you not to think of this as a rigid method or list to be repeated, but as reminders of truth that you hold dear and cherish. The freedom to share what is on your mind and heart will become more natural and less like making a presentation that you have prepared. Your God talk will become more natural and less rehearsed as you speak with God and man.

Section III
The Actions of God

9
God's Action in Creating

> *Memory Hook – The memory hook for God's action in creating is to cup both hands together as if making a snowball.*

Why are the Actions of God Important? God reveals himself as a God of action. His actions have great significance for us and we should pay close attention to what he has done, is currently doing and has promised to do in the future. In this section we will survey five actions that everyone should understand and be able to talk about. We could certainly list more than five, but in our desire to present an outline that is easily remembered and hits the highlights, we will limit our list to these.

Why is speaking about God's action important? Several reasons stand out. First, it speaks to God's purpose in the world. Many today believe that the universe is random, that life is ruled by chance. This explanation it not very satisfying, but it is necessary when you exclude God from your worldview. You are left with an accidental universe of change. Second, it provides purpose and meaning for life. If your life is in line with God's purposes and you live in a manner consistent with God's character and you understand the purposes of his actions, then life becomes meaningful beyond immediate gratification and materialism. This is something the world desperately needs today. Third, God's actions speak directly to our basic human sinfulness and need for salvation. Fourth, it is often in understanding God's gracious actions that we first begin to see something of his glory.

God's action in providing salvation needs to be anchored in the context of God's character. This is true of all his activity in the world. All of his actions make more sense when viewed in light of his nature and perfections. Separating his salvation work from his other works and his character diminishes it urgency and greatness. It will weaken the impact of the magnificent story of redemption. I believe that the Holy Spirit is interested in disclosing the whole truth about God and man. Too often, however, we act as if we are marketing just a few selected benefits of the gospel. This is another reason it is important to broaden our God talk and trust the Holy Spirit to disclose who God is to a person's heart and mind.

When opportunity presents itself, I recommend that you bear witness to a wider picture of God and what he has done. Summarize. Then stop and expand on a specific area. Then summarize again. You can return to the main sweeping themes of your God talk by saying, "I think it is important to see what we are talking about in the context of Who God is. May I share with you a short overview of what I have learned about God from the Bible? I think it would help clarify what we are talking about."

Let us now proceed with the first of five important actions of God: God's action in creating. The Bible boldly states, "In the beginning God created the heavens and the earth."[96] It is not apologetic or defensive, and we should not be either. The Bible does not always tell us all that we would like to know. It was not written to satisfy our curiosity. It does, however, contain what God has deemed important for us to know. It states clearly again and again that God took creative action. "The Lord God made the earth and the heavens... the Lord God formed the man from the dust of the ground and breathed into his nostrils the breath of life, and the man became a living being." "When God created man, he made him in the likeness of God. He created them male and female."[97] Isaiah continues, "This is what God the Lord says – he who created the heavens and stretched them out, who spread out the earth and all that comes out of it, who gives breath to its people, and life to those who walk on it." And later, "It is I who made the earth and created mankind upon it. My own hands stretched out the heavens ...this is what the Lord says – he who created the heavens, he is God; he who fashioned and made the earth, he founded it; he did not create it to be empty, but formed it to be inhabited."[98]

Jesus spoke of the account of creation as fact.[99] John tells us that Jesus was not only present at creation but that he personally was actively taking action and that nothing was made without him.[100] Paul also states that "all things were created by him."[101]

In the Old Testament David says that the creation demonstrates God's glory and speaks about "the work of his hands."[102] In the New Testament, Paul picks up this idea of

---

97   Genesis 2:4, 7; 5:1-2
98   Isaiah 42:5; 45:12; 18
99   Mark 10:6
100   John 1:3
101   Colossians 1:16
102   Psalm 19:1-4

the creation being a clear witness to the nature of God that leaves men without an excuse for unbelief.[103] We can see that God's action in creation is vitally important in bearing witness about God. We should not shy away from speaking about it because it is not popular to do so in our day of skeptical and cynical thinking.

God did not stop creating after the original work was finished. A future new heaven and new earth are yet in store.[104] Jesus spoke of his present creative work in preparation for this future place when he said, "I am going there to prepare a place for you."[105]

The New Testament speaks of another work of creation; a new creation, a spiritual creation that God is bringing about through the creative work of the Holy Spirit.[106] Just as the Spirit was involved in the original creative action of God, he is now involved in bringing about the new creation of spiritual life.

The creation activity of God is central to what God has done, is currently doing and will yet do in the future. We must include God's action in creating as part of our God talk.

---

103   Romans 1:19-20
104   Revelation 21:1
105   John 14:2
106   2 Corinthians 5:17-18; Galatians 6:15; John 3:3-8;
2 Corinthians 3:6

10
God's Action in Sustaining

Memory Hook - The memory hook for God's sustaining action is to open the hands from the cupped position in a holding/protecting motion with one hand under and the other alongside. God holds, sustains, protects, guides and provides shelter.

God's activity of sustaining takes many forms. The Apostle Paul links together Jesus' role in creating and sustaining the universe and says that, "in him all things hold together."[107] If we are to take this literally (as many believe) we could conclude that the universe would self-destruct if it were not for God's sustaining action. The worldview presented in the Bible reveals that God is cosmically active not passive in his relationship with the universe. He upholds and sustains it. Many people today assume that God is passive, distant and uninvolved. They have adopted a naturalistic worldview without seriously considering the biblical evidence.

It is one thing to think about the sustaining work of God in the universe, but quite another to realize that God sustains individuals. It is here that the Bible springs to

---

107   Colossians 1:17

life with personal application. David's testimony rang out clearly. "The Lord was my support."[108] He spoke to others and instructed them to live by this principle that, "the Lord upholds the righteous" and that they too should cast their troubles on the Lord because, "he will sustain you."[109]

The truth that God is actively supporting, sustaining, guiding, providing and protecting his children is a very precious thought that is important to communicate. Many who are suffering through difficult times are longing to know that God is not detached, passive and distant, but active and personally involved in upholding them.

The Psalms are rich in sustaining/protecting language. "Blessed are all who take refuge in him... let all who take refuge in you be glad... Spread your protection over them, that those who love your name may rejoice in you... Show the wonder of your great love, you who save by your right hand those who take refuge in you... The Lord is my rock, my fortress and my deliverer; my God is my rock, in whom I take refuge. He is my shield and the horn of my salvation, my stronghold... In the shelter of your presence you hide them... I long to dwell in your tent forever and take refuge in the shelter of your wings... He who dwells in the shelter of the Most High will rest in the shadow of the Almighty... If the Lord delights in a man's way, he makes his steps firm; though he stumble, he will not fall, for the Lord upholds him with his hand."[110]

One could also include the guiding language that is so commonly used under this heading of the sustaining work of God. "He guides me in paths of righteousness for his name's sake... I will instruct you and teach you in the way

108   2 Samuel 22:19
109   Psalm 37:17; 55:22
110   Psalm 2:12; 5:11; 17:7; 18:2; 31:20; 61:4; 91:1; 37:23-24

you should go; I will counsel you and watch over you."[111] Paul made a wonderful statement of God's supply to the Philippian believers, "And my God will meet all your needs according to his glorious riches in Christ Jesus."[112]

God is active today sustaining, guiding, upholding, protecting and supplying the needs of his people.

111   Psalm 23:3; 32:8
112   Philippians 4:19

11
God's Action in Redeeming

> *Memory Hook - The memory hook for God's action in redeeming is to curve the fingers and touch them to the palm of the hand. This reminds us of the nails that were used to pierce Jesus' hands on the cross and provides a fitting symbol of redemption.*

The theme of redemption permeates the Bible. God's action in redeeming a people for his own is (from our human perspective) his greatest work. It centers in the cross of Jesus Christ but is anticipated throughout the Old Testament. God carefully laid a foundation that pointed forward to the cross. The story of redemption is depicted symbolically on Mount Moriah when Abraham is told to sacrifice his son Isaac. Then God intervened at the last moment and provided a substitute sacrifice.[113]

Prominent in the Old Testament is God's redeeming action to bring his people out of slavery in Egypt. The Passover lamb was killed as a substitute for the first born son of each household.[114] This event is celebrated throughout the Old Testament in song, story and ritual. The sacrificial

---

113   Genesis 22:1-19
114   Exodus 12-13:16

offerings of Jewish worship explained in great detail in the book of Leviticus point forward to the cross of Jesus Christ where his blood was shed for cleansing from sin. Embedded in the stories of Ruth and Job is the concept of a redeemer.[115] Redeemer language is also used in the story of Jeremiah buying (redeeming) from his cousin Hanamel a plot of land for an inheritance.[116] In the book of Isaiah God is mentioned as the Redeemer of Israel thirteen times.[117] Also, God's action of redeeming Judah from Babylon is a significant theme for understanding the message of the Old Testament prophets.

The central subject of the New Testament is the life, death and resurrection of Jesus Christ. His work in providing salvation is spoken of as his redemptive work on the cross on behalf of sinners.[118] Paul repeatedly returns to this important theme. "Christ redeemed us from the curse of the law by becoming a curse for us... He redeemed us in order that the blessing given to Abraham might come to the Gentiles through Christ Jesus, so that by faith we might receive the promise of the Spirit."[119] His work took place at the precise time in history planned by God to provide the believer the full rights of being sons as opposed to slaves.[120] It provides a wonderful hope for those who wait for his glorious return and the motivation to live pure lives and to do the good work that he has for them to do.[121] Peter adds

---

115   Ruth 4:14; Job 19:25
116   Jeremiah 32:6-15
117   Isaiah 41:14; 43:1; 44:6; 24; 47:4; 48:17; 49:7, 26; 54:5, 8; 59:20; 60:16; 63:16
118   1 Corinthians 1:18, 23; 2:2; Romans 3:21-25
119   Galatians 3:13-14
120   Galatians 4:4-7
121   Titus 2:13-14; Ephesians 2:10

his voice to this redemption theme and calls the believer to live in reverent fear before God because of the precious blood of Christ that paid for it.[122]

Telling the redemption story is important God talk. It needs to be shared, not in isolation, but in the context of who God is.

12
God's Action of Inviting

> *Memory Hook – The memory hook for God's action of inviting individuals to come to him through Jesus is open hands stretched outward. In reality it is Jesus' hands that are open to the sinner inviting those who hear and believe to come to him.*

In the Old Testament, God's action of inviting is found primarily in the context of the covenant people of God. We see the Lord inviting his people to come, listen, repent, be cleansed and worship.[123] This is often expressed as an invitation to taste and experience that the Lord is good.[124] It is pictured as being bread from heaven to eat or living water to drink.[125] The promise is straightforward and clear - if you respond to the invitation you will live and enjoy a soul satisfying relationship with the God of heaven. The Psalms often frame the invitation as one of coming to God for the purpose of worship, to acknowledge who God is and delight in his awesome presence.[126]

---

123   Isaiah 48:14, 16; 1:18
124   Psalm 34:8
125   Isaiah 55:1-3
126   Psalm 100:2

In the New Testament we observe the disciples called to follow Jesus.[127] The crowds are challenged through the preaching of John the Baptist to repent and be baptized.[128] Jesus preached a message of invitation to repent and believe that was addressed to sinners, the weary and spiritually thirsty.[129] This invitation is repeated and generalized by the Holy Spirit and the church at the very end of the Bible. "The Spirit and the bride say, 'Come!' And let him who hears say, 'Come!' Whoever is thirsty, let him come; and whoever wishes, let him take the free gift of the water of life."[130]

This wonderful and mysterious invitation in the New Testament is framed on one side by God's eternal sovereign call upon a person by the Father, and on the other by the individual's responsibility to respond in faith.[131] From the human perspective, we must respond to the invitation to believe the good news of the gospel that Jesus is who he claimed to be, the eternal Son of God, and that his death on the cross was God's provision for one's personal sin and guilt. It is an invitation that Paul says demands a response, "That if you confess with your mouth, 'Jesus is Lord,' and believe in your heart that God raised him from the dead, you will be saved. For it is with your heart that you believe and are justified, and it is with your mouth that you confess and are saved." He summarizes the invitation with these words, "Everyone who calls on the name of the Lord will be saved."[132]

---

127   Matthew 4:19
128   Matthew 3:2,6
129   Matthew 4:17; 9:13, 11:28-30; John 7:37-38
130   Revelation 22:17
131   John 1:12-13; 6:37, 44, 46
132   Romans 10:9-10, 13

We are to proclaim the good news of God's invitation realizing that it is God who is at work taking action to call people to himself.

13
God's Action of Judging

> *Memory Hook - The memory hook for God's action in judging is a closed fist. God's judgment is like a hammer or a rock that crushes all who fall under its weight.*

The good news of God's work of inviting is warm, positive and popular. We must, however, be faithful to include another major theme of the Bible that is not so popular, that of God's judgment. Many prefer to leave this out of their God talk. It seems out of step with today's politically correct, inclusive and man-centered spirit. It seems too harsh and old fashioned, a message more for the Puritans from another time and place. But it is relevant today if we are to be balanced and present a more complete and accurate picture of who God is. There is no hope in escaping the judgment of God apart from embracing God's provision of his Son, the Savior, who has already carried God's judgment as our substitute on the cross.

David says boldly, "The Lord reigns forever; he has established his throne for judgment. He will judge the world in righteousness."[133] He also says, "The wicked will

---

133   Psalm 9:7-8

not stand in the judgment."[134] There are three important facts in these verses (1) God is sovereign, he reigns eternally (2) God's judgment of the world will be righteous and (3) the unrighteous will not stand. If this is true (and the Bible clearly says that it is) then it makes the truth about God's actions in redemption and invitation even more wonderful, and essentially important for us to talk about. The message of the cross is, as we have already seen, about Jesus bearing the wrath of God that we deserve. It is important to see God's action of judging in the context of the five clusters of the perfections of God. God's righteous actions spring from and are always consistent with his righteous character.

In the Old Testament the judgment of God is often viewed collectively within the context the nation Israel (and surrounding nations) and the covenant God had made with his people through Moses. There were clear promises of blessing for obedience and curses for disobedience as stated in Deuteronomy chapter 28. As the history of Israel unfolded this theme is central and important to remember. The prophets spoke about the nation's obedience and disobedience. They reminded the people of God's promise to both bless and bring judgment.[135] At times the prophets looked into the distant future and spoke of God's final judgment and blessing.[136] As the nation Israel failed again and again the theme of God's judgment is pervasive but future grace is promised through a new covenant that will provide a new heart that will make obedience possible.[137]

---

134   Psalm 1:5
135   Isaiah 5:1-30
136   Isaiah 66:15-16, 22
137   Jeremiah 31:31-34

In the New Testament the cross is central, and with it the coming of the new covenant promised through Jeremiah and fulfilled in Jesus' blood.[138] God's judgment and wrath were poured out on the cross. His wrath was propitiated (turned away) and the believer's sin covered. Those who have been united with Christ stand before God justified (declared not guilty) in Jesus Christ and robed in his righteousness.[139]

The theme of God's coming judgment upon the unbelieving nations and individuals is an important theme in the Bible. The writer of the book of Hebrews says that, "man is destined to die once, and after that to face judgment."[140]

In the book of Revelation we observe an angel announcing (at some time in the future) that the time of God's judgment has arrived.[141] At that appointed time God's wrath will be poured out upon the earth and the nations in both unusual and severe ways. Rather that worshipping God, most of the earth's population will curse God and try to hide from him. This time of general judgment (tribulation) is followed by a final personal judgment (for all unbelievers) before the sovereign, holy and righteous God of heaven and earth. What happens at this judgment is stated clearly in Scripture. "Then I saw a great white throne and him who was seated on it. Earth and sky fled from his presence, and there was no place for them. And I saw the dead, great and small, standing before the throne, and books were opened. Another book was opened, which is the book of life. The dead were judged according to what they had done as recorded in the books. The sea gave up the dead that were in

---

138   1 Corinthians 11:25
139   Romans 4:22-25; 5:1; 6:6
140   Hebrews 9:27
141   Revelation 14:7

it, and death and Hades gave up the dead that were in them, and each person was judged according to what he had done. Then death and Hades were thrown into the lake of fire. The lake of fire is the second death. If anyone's name was not found written in the book of life, he was thrown into the lake of fire."[142] It is clear that having one's name written in the book of life (another way of speaking about those who have eternal life in Christ) is the most important part of this vision of God's final action of judgment. It appears that the books that are opened containing the records of people's deeds are used to show that the verdict of guilty is justified and that these individuals without Christ have no hope.

---

142   Revelation 20:11-15

Section IV
Private Worship

Private God Talk:
Celebrating the Attributes and Actions of God

Private worship can and should be both structured and unstructured. It is good to linger in the presence of the Lord with no other agenda but to adore him. At these times of unstructured fellowship we can allow the Holy Spirit to set the direction of our thoughts, following his lead regarding the subject flow of our time in prayer and praise.

It is also good, at times, to use something to guide our thoughts; a form to structure our time of worship. There are many ways to do this. Working through a list of the names of God can be helpful. Dick Eastman's book, The Hour That Changes the World, on how to pray for an hour, is a great way to start by dividing the hour into segments.[143] Let's return to the subject introduced at the end of chapter eight and develop it further. It is logical to expand your time of private worship to include both the perfections of God and his glorious actions. As previously stated it is important to see the actions of God anchored in and consistent with the attributes of God. I believe that rehearsing them in our time of private praise and worship is good.

Let me illustrate how a time of personal worship might look and feel. While moving my hands through the motions of the memory hooks I might say, "I praise you Father, Son and Holy Spirit for being above and beyond the creation. You are the only true and living God. You are the Almighty existing eternally in three persons in perfect harmony and communion. I praise you for being a personal God who is interested in relating to me as an individual. Thank you that I can share my thoughts and feelings with you and that you see all I do. Help me to please you in all of life. Thank you

---

143   Dick Eastman, *The Hour That Changes The World*
(Grand Rapids: Baker Books, 1978).

for speaking in the Scriptures and for sending Jesus Christ to be my Savior and for providing the Holy Spirit to be with me and in me. Thank you for his illuminating work in making the Bible come alive to me. Thank you for inviting me to fellowship with you."

I may pause to grasp my thumb with my opposite hand and begin to rejoice in the various aspects of God's sovereignty and how God deals with me in his sovereignty. I reflect on his providence and rule over all things including the details of each day. "Lord I bow to your sovereignty and give you worship and praise as Almighty God. I praise you for your righteousness, holiness and justice. Thank you for your love, kindness and compassion that you focus upon me in Christ. I am reminded of the purity of your love and the limitless dimensions of your compassion for me." I pause to pray Paul's prayer found in Ephesians 3:14-21 and remind myself of how he thought about God's love. Moving on to how God has expressed his love in making promises as the covenant keeping God I express my thanksgiving to him for being faithful and trustworthy. I next turn my attention to his grace and mercy that was poured out upon me while I was weak and powerless to help myself. "Father, I thank you for your grace and mercy to me."

Moving on to reflect on the beauty and wonder of the creation I might say; "Thank you, Lord for creating the beauty of the sky, the mountains, the trees and the sea. I praise you for the new creation of life in the Spirit and the new heavens and new earth that is yet to be revealed and that you are preparing a place for me that will be wonderful because you are there. Thank you for sustaining me during this present time when I am vulnerable while living is this fallen world." Curling my fingers into my palm I continue, "Thank you Lord for the redemption that I have in Christ and for saving me from my slavery to sin." Opening my hands and stretching them out I say, "Thank you for your calling me to yourself and for providing the grace to respond in faith to your invitation." Turning my hand into a fist I pray, "Come quickly Lord Jesus. I long for you to establish justice on the earth and bringing in the visible reign of your righteousness and glory. I pray for those who are not ready for that day but will face your coming judgment and pray that your grace and mercy will be extended to them before it is too late."

This can be expanded almost without limit as you explore the actions and attributes of God. More and more passages of Scripture will come to mind as you read the Bible and expand your ability to roam throughout the major themes of Scripture. Your time of worship will deepen as you broaden your understanding of God's perfections and actions. At the same time you are becoming better prepared to share your God talk with others. Your witness about God will become richer, more alive and seem more natural. The Holy Spirit will continue to add new dimensions as he equips you to speak of the glories of the attributes and actions of God to you as you explore the Scriptures.

We are called to enjoy him as we learn to walk in his presence. David's testimony should give us hope to explore and expand our personal time with God. "Surely you have granted him eternal blessings and made him glad with the joy of your presence. For the king trusts in the Lord; through the unfailing love of the Most High he will not be shaken."[144]

I pray that you will find new dimensions of joy in God's presence as you develop your God talk.

---

144   Psalm 21:6-7

Section V
The Church and Strategic Equipping

Is Equipping Viewed as Strategic?

"Let the professionals do the God talk. They speak so much better than us laymen. They are trained and we are not." Historically the gravitational force has been consistently downward and away from the biblical pattern that God has provided and gifted a few to equip the many.[145] Most churches give lip service to the need for equipping but it is difficult to find many examples where it is taken seriously. Concrete results of actual laymen being equipped and confidently witnessing are sparse. Unfortunately in the Western developed world both clergy and laity contribute to perpetuating the miss-belief that professionals do God talk better. In areas of the world where there are great movements of people coming to Christ, laypeople are active in talking about God within their relational networks.

It is time for the clergy and laity to develop a re-energized and focused partnership to accomplish the task of equipping every believer for effective God talk. This will demand a new attitude, fresh vision and possibly tackling some current deficits within the church.

I believe that there remains in the church a shallow understanding of who God is. J. I. Packer put it bluntly in his classic book Knowing God when he wrote, "ignorance of God ... lies at the root of much of the church's weakness today."[146] If you ask the average church attendee to describe God they will likely fumble and stumble groping to find words. The truth is that we struggle to put into simple words

---

145   Ephesians 4:11-12
146   J. I. Packer, *Knowing God*
(Downers Grove, IL: InterVarsity Press, 1973), p.6.

what we say we believe about God. Fuzzy thinking is hard to articulate. We must seriously address the lack of interest and mastery of our basic theology of God.

We should also re-examine our evangelism strategies. Worship celebration is important for the church but is it the most effective method of evangelism? Many churches invest heavily in special event evangelism designed to bring people to a program at the church. Christmas and Easter are two wonderful times for the church to celebrate the coming of the Messiah and his death and resurrection. It is true that these are great opportunities to speak about God, and God has graciously used them in the work of evangelism. As competition for attention in the public square becomes increasingly intense. Churches often respond by spending escalating amounts of energy and resources on more professional quality music, lighting and dramatic presentations that carry as much glitter as their budget and talent can muster. A theater model of evangelism, however, does little to equip believers to engage in personal God talk beyond "that was a really cool program" or "the music was inspiring." In reality, these events can be counterproductive to empowering laymen to speak unless they are coupled with specific training to use the event to launch private personal conversations. The reason I suggest it may be counterproductive is that it inadvertently trains the foot soldiers of the church to be passive observers.

The church is left exhausted from the production of these special events that give little thought or energy to the equipping of their people to speak more effectively as individuals. On the positive side, the holiday seasons do (at least for a few brief moments) shed light on the miracle of the incarnation and the resurrection. The demands of time and schedule pressure us to quickly tell as much of the gospel story as possible before the crowd hurries on to the next holiday activity. Ultimately, effective communication about God remains a real challenge amid the countless distractions that dazzle and glitter in 3D and jingle in surround sound. Too often we are left with an abbreviated summary and undersized view of God.

While all of this activity is taking place, many Christians suffer quiet guilt, intimidated to speak. They find it safer to support these public programs than attempt to speak a private word of witness to a friend or neighbor. Speaking about the gospel and God in a more comprehensive way seems beyond the grasp. The zealous few who try to find their voice uneasily memorize lines that tend to come across as unnatural and stiff. No matter how hard they try, it does not seem to have a clear and convincing ring of personal conviction and authenticity. We know that we need to become better equipped to speak about God beyond pat answers and clever slogans, but we have been left a little jaded and possibly a bit cynical by some of the mass-marketing evangelistic campaigns that have come and gone. If we are honest we must concede that these well-meaning but thin attempts have done little to stimulate real conversations or helped us communicate effectively.

Some have turned away from the importance of communicating the content of the gospel in words, and instead promote warm personal experiences, artistic impressions and symbolic images. There has been noticeable interest by some evangelicals in the mystical (what some have cleverly tagged as "smells and bells"). Accoutrements in worship may have their place, but are they the best way to communicate the message of the gospel? I see several risks that must be considered. First, this approach seems to follow the logic that if we provide the right emotional atmosphere people will be moved emotionally to respond to the gospel. Placing undue emphasis on slick religious staging for the purpose of promoting a metaphysical experience sounds manipulative and dishonest. Second, it plays into the hands of post-modern pluralism - that knowing universal truth is a lost cause and that personal experience trumps doctrinal content. The New Testament writers believed that the content of the "faith that was once for all entrusted to the saints" was important to guard and we are instructed to contend for it.[147] Speaking truth continues to be important no matter what the distractions or current trends.

Doctrine and theology have fallen on hard times in many circles. Even use of these words is avoided. Some feel that they tend to promote division rather than unity, while others think that they are just out of step with the average person's interests. Since this book is about aiding average believers to communicate doctrine and theology, let me respond with a simple defense.

Theology is simply the study of God. Doctrine is organizing the truth that we have gained in our study of God into a logical sequence that we can communicate. Every believer needs to know basic truth about God and be able to organize it in his or her mind well enough to communicate it without notes to another person. The aim of this book is to equip the average person to do just that. It is time that church leaders re-examine their local strategy and performance in this basic mandate to equip the average layman to witness with more robust God talk.

---

147   Jude 1:3

Toward a Better Understanding of the Role of Distress

When we encounter people in distress, our first response is usually to do what we can to provide relief. This is good, noble and biblical, but our thinking about distress needs to be stretched. God talk during times of distress can be risky, yet richly rewarding. Discomfort, pain and suffering are universal, but uniquely personal, ranging from minor irritant to painful paralysis. Relevant God talk must be sensitive to the individual's experience and have a good theology of distress.

Medical literature speaks about distress in a technical way. It is referred to as a negative state of failure to cope with stress (a maladaptive response that diminishes functioning) or to the heightened emotional reaction caused by a stressful event (a stressor). This may be true and helpful for the academic, but it leaves God out of the picture. What does distress have to do with God? What is God doing in this uncomfortable situation? To dialogue with a person about these questions we must start with a better understanding of what the Bible teaches about distress.

The word distress is used broadly in both Old and New Testaments and deserves careful attention. The English word distress is found only 83 times, but when we search the nearly 20 Greek and Hebrew words behind it, the use jumps to over 450 times. If the search is expanded to include related words (like sorrow) we discovers a vast subject that demands our study.

The biblical writers speak about distress in three general categories; (1) external events that are distressful, often descriptions of people being in circumstances of trouble or straits of some kind, (2) the distress caused by God's hand of judgment, sometimes past and sometimes pointing to a future time of great trouble or tribulation that is predicted to come upon the world that will produce great distress and (3) the emotional feelings of distress that people experience internally.

A few examples might be helpful. Jacob felt emotional distress due to having conflict with others and from having an encounter with God.[148] David experienced emotional distress during a stressful situation and "found strength in the Lord his God."[149] The Psalms provide 17 specific examples of distress (where the word distress is used).[150] Six are prayers that cry out for relief from distress; ten are expressions of worship, testimony or thanksgiving for having received relief from distress. Almost half are attributed to David.

In Moses' sermon in Deuteronomy he prophesied that God would bring distress upon the covenant people Israel for their disobedience and then foretold how he would use it to bring them to repentance.[151] Moses also told how God used distress to harden the heart of Pharaoh when the Israelites were brought out of Egypt.[152]

The book of Judges records a pattern of repeated cycles demonstrating God's use of distress to bring the people to a point of repentance from sin and to cry out to God for

---

148   Genesis 28:17; 32:7; 35:3

149   1 Samuel 30:6

150   Psalm 4:1; 18:6; 25:17; 31:9; 35:26; 59:16; 66:14; 69:17; 71:20; 102:2; 106:44; 107:6, 13, 19, 28; 116:3; 118:5

151   Deuteronomy 4:27-31; 28:45-68

152   Deuteronomy 6:22

relief.[153] In the book of Ruth, Naomi assumes God's hand of judgment is upon her when her husband and two sons die in Moab and she says, "Call me Mara, because the Almighty has made my life very bitter" and "The Lord has afflicted me; the Almighty has brought misfortune upon me."[154]

In First Samuel we discover a number of examples of the writer contrasting godly and ungodly reactions to distress.[155] Hannah, in distress, poured out her heart to God in prayer. The word distress is used in the prophecy regarding the coming judgment on Eli's family. When God accused the people of rejecting his leadership by demanding a king, God described himself as the One "who saves you out of all your calamities and distresses." The text says Samuel was distressed when God disclosed to him, "I am grieved that I have made Saul king" and "he cried out to the Lord all that night." The writer records that those who were distressed joined David, God's anointed future king. David expressed hope in God's deliverance and found strength in the Lord when experiencing distress in contrast to Saul when he was approaching the end of his life and expressed the words, "I am in great distress."

Amnon worked himself into a state of emotional distress succumbing to the temptation of lust and sexual sin. This is contrasted with David rejoicing in God's deliverance and looking to God's mercy even when he sinned by counting the fighting men.[156]

The concept of distress permeates the writings of the prophets. Typically it is viewed as caused by God's hand

---

153   Judges 2:15; 10:9,14
154   Ruth 1:13; 20-21
155   1 Samuel 1:10; 2:32; 10:19; 15:10-11; 22:2; 26:24; 30:6; 28:15
156   2 Samuel 13:2; 2 Samuel 22:17-20; 24:14

of judgment and frequently involved opposing armies to punish Israel, Judah or other nations for their sin.[157] In Haggai chapter one the Lord's message to the post-exile people makes it clear that it is God's action that brought economic difficulty, poor harvests and monetary inflation (all forms of distress) to the people.

---

157   Isaiah 5:30; Jeremiah 19:9

General Conclusions

1. God, in his sovereignty, graciously uses external and internal distress to call people to himself. He desires that people in distress cry out to him in repentance for his help and salvation.

2. God, in his mercy, helps those who call out to him in times of distress.[158] He sustains and strengthens those who ask in faith and submit to him. He enables them to endure times of distress and sometimes rescues them by providing other interventions, but always desires that they have an eternal perspective.[159]

3. God, in his justice, inflicts judgment (causing distress) upon some people and nations, for his own purposes (sometimes to harden hearts, sometimes to reveal truth, punish or purge sin, sometimes to purify his people, to name just a few).

4. God, in his love, compassion and grace, has provided justice for sin through Christ's sacrifice on the cross paying the penalty for the sins of those who believe on his name. He is faithful to keep the promises he has made and recorded in his word.[160]

5. God is faithful to use distress to discipline his children for the purpose of holiness.[161]

---

158   Matthew 11:28-29

159   Hebrews 11

160   Romans 3:22-26; Matthew 5:18

161   Romans 8:28-30; Hebrews 12:4-11; James 1:2-4, 12; 1 Peter 1:6-7, 15-17

6. God's temporal judgments always warn of and foreshadow his final coming judgment and point to the suffering of eternal distress.[162]

7. God's wrath is currently being revealed as God allows sin's natural consequences to be experienced causing various forms of distress.[163]

8. Man's experiences of distress can often be traced back to living in a manner that is inconsistent with or violates the perfections of God. These experiences of distress provide opportunity to point people back to the attributes of God and work of Christ for relief and salvation.

9. Not all emotional distress is sinful. Jesus (the sinless Redeemer) experienced distress on several occasions, Gethsemane and Golgotha being the most extreme.[164] The ability to feel emotion is just one aspect of man being created in the image of God.

---

162   Isaiah 65:14; Matthew 13:42; Luke 13:1-5
163   Romans 1:18
164   Matthew 26:36; Luke 22:44; John 19:17-18

Implications for Evangelism

1. We need to be more proactive in training God's people to think and speak about distress before it occurs. We need to cultivate a more biblical worldview that puts God at the center of things and better understands the relationship between human events, personal distress and how individuals relate to God within the context of his person and his activity in the world.

2. We need to model (live out and demonstrate before a watching world) and be able to articulate how individuals were created to relate to the Creator-God in daily life (in ways that are consistent with each of the five clusters of the perfections of God). We need to live a balanced life in relation to these clusters and therefore reflect who God is in a healthy way.

3. We need to be ready to speak about the gospel (the person and redemptive work of Jesus Christ) in the context of a person's current worldview and build bridges that transition to a biblical worldview.

4. We need to be sensitive to the pain and discomfort that distress brings, showing compassion and understanding while beginning the dialogue (in cooperation with the work of the Holy Spirit) to gently confront individuals with a better understanding of the attributes and actions of God.

5. We need to be ready to tell our testimony of what God has done for us.

6. We need to be ready to tell the storyline of how God has worked in the lives of other real people (both biblical and contemporary).

7. We need to realize that God is at work during times of distress without running ahead of him, lagging behind and missing opportunities. We must avoid making promises to people in distress that mislead (i.e. guaranteeing that God will remove current distress). When there is no indication of internal distress (conviction of sin) it raises questions about the Holy Spirit's activity. It is his role to produce genuine conviction of sin that leads to repentance. It may be advisable to sow seed-thoughts and wait, rather than push ahead trying to "close a sale."

The purpose of this section is to serve as an introductory survey. These brief conclusions are offered in the hopes that it will stimulate additional thinking that is needed on this important biblical theme and that the church will develop a more defined theology of distress.

Growing Deep Conviction about Truth

Conviction to speak about God is enhanced by confidence that what we are speaking is true. This comes from the study of the Holy Scriptures. Unfortunately we are exposed to much sloppy God talk today that misuses the Bible. Listening to impassioned, smooth talking or clever preaching does not provide long-term conviction or confidence for laymen to speak about God. Secondhand conviction is short-lived. It can even have the opposite effect and dampen the willingness of laymen to speak. Being exposed to preaching that has much heat but little light will, over time, breed insecurity about what is true. Every Christian should be equipped to understand how to do solid Bible study. This will help him or her to better discern truth about God and build personal conviction to speak to others. Permit me to pass along some brief comments that hopefully will be helpful in building an equipping foundation in the local church.

First, we should remember that truth is knowable. We live in a day of postmodern pluralism that says everyone's opinion or belief is private and only valid for them. The existence of universal truth is denied and if it did exist would be unknowable. But as believers in the Creator-God who has spoken in his Son Jesus Christ and in the Scriptures,[165] we believe that God's revelation in the Bible is trustworthy, true and knowable.[166] We should speak with confident boldness yet with humility and gentleness to those who have lost hope and are confused by hearing many conflicting opinions. We must faithfully point people to the God of the Bible and the truth that he has revealed. Carson reminds us that pluralism

165   Hebrews 1:1-2
166   2 Timothy 3:16

demands changes in hermeneutics (how to study).[167] We must be aware of the dangerous trend today that shifts the authority away from the text to the one reading the text. We must continue to place ourselves under the authority of the Scriptures in all that we do.

Second, we should keep our balance between biblical theology and systematic theology. They should inform and guard each other and should not be done in isolation. Biblical theology asks questions of the meaning of the text. Systematic theology asks summary questions like; "What is God?" If systematic theology picks verses from Scripture to prove or support a point but has not done the work of biblical theology that accurately exegetes the text it will abuse and misuse the Bible and build on an invalid foundation. The material in *God Talk* is systematic theology. It assumes that biblical theology was done on every reference used. We need to be diligent to do good accurate work in both our biblical theology and our systematic theology.

Let me outline for you a method of interpreting the Bible (using the methods of biblical theology) that I have used for over 35 years. I learned this from Walter C. Kaiser, Jr. to whom I am indebted for helping me learn how to approach Scripture. Kaiser served as academic dean and vice president of education and professor at Trinity Evangelical Divinity School and later as president of Gordon Conwell Seminary. The hermeneutical method he taught was simple and easy to use. It has helped me immensely and I am very grateful for his impact on my ministry. I can still hear him admonishing the class with one of his frequent statements, "Keep your finger on the text."

Here is a brief summary of that method.

---

167   D. A. Carson,
The Gagging of God: Christianity Confronts Pluralism
(Grand Rapids, Zondervan, 1996).

How to Study The Bible

The three tasks of Bible study are to find...

1. The Meaning
2. The Principle
3. The Application

The Meaning: There is only one meaning of a biblical text. It is the intended meaning of the author for those he was addressing. The five tools that we use for finding the meaning of the text are:

1. Historical Setting
2. Main Idea
3. Context
4. Words and Sentences
5. Harmony with Other Scriptures

The Principle: The principle is the biblical truth stated in a simple statement that bridges the years from "then" (when the author wrote) to "now" (the present day). Other terms to describe this are: lesson, teaching, significance and implication.

The Application: Personal application is taking biblical truth, making it yours and acting upon it.

Conclusion

This book is a call to action. In simple language it is a challenge to speak up with a more robust message about God. Section Five explored implications for those charged with the task of equipping the Church to take action. While pastors and teachers have a special and sacred resonsibility to train every believer to speak more effectively about God, every Christian should be encouraged to have meaningful conversations about God.

Don't let fear keep you on the sidelines, get in the game. The Bible does alert us to the fact that God talk is often costly. You may be misunderstood, marginalized or even persecuted for speaking about the Living God who places demands upon the life of every individual.

Some are called to go to difficult distant places in the world that demand crossing cultural and language barriers. For you, that hard place may be across the street or speaking to a friend or family member. Wherever your God talk takes you, be assured that Jesus has promised to be present with us and to empower us with his Holy Spirit to be his witnesses. May God encourage you to expand your God talk as you take bold steps and speak up.